GRATIAS

GRATIAS

A Little Book of Gratitude

Compiled by John Quinn

VERITAS

Published 2018 by
Veritas Publications
7–8 Lower Abbey Street
Dublin 1, Ireland

publications@veritas.ie
www.veritas.ie

ISBN 978-1-84730-860-3

10 9 8 7 6 5 4

Book design by Lir Mac Cárthaigh
Printed in Ireland by
Anglo Printers Ltd, Drogheda

*Veritas books are printed on paper
made from the wood pulp of managed
forests. For every tree felled, at least
one tree is planted, thereby renewing
natural resources.*

The lines from 'This, My Everyday',
'Thoughts' and 'Thanksgiving' by
Mary Redmond are reprinted from
The Pink Ribbon Path, Dublin: The
Columba Press, 2013. Used with
kind permission.

The lines from 'Question to
Life', 'The Long Garden' and
'Ploughman' by Patrick Kavanagh
are reprinted from *Collected Poems*,
edited by Antoinette Quinn (Allen
Lane, 2004), by kind permission
of the Trustees of the Estate of
the late Katherine B. Kavanagh,
through the Jonathan Williams
Literary Agency.

The lines from 'Album' by Seamus
Heaney are reprinted from *Human
Chain* (2010), and the lines from
'While all the other were away at
Mass', 'Clearances III' are reprinted
from *Open Ground* (1998), both
published by Faber and Faber Ltd.
Used with permission.

The lines from 'The Peace of Wild
Things' by Wendell Berry are
reprinted from *The Selected Poems
of Wendell Berry*, Berkeley, CA:
Counterpoint Press, 1999. Used
with permission.

The lines from *Nostos: An
Autobiography* by John Moriarty
(2011) are reprinted by permission
of the Lilliput Press of Dublin.

Contents

Dedicated to the memory of
MARY REDMOND

'The best form of giving is thanksgiving.'

Foreword

It may be a clichéd beginning to a book about gratitude to say that I am *grateful* to John Quinn for the opportunity to write the foreword to his book. It is not the first time I have had the honour of writing a foreword to a work of his and on each occasion I have struggled to capture adequately, the essence and profundity of his observations and reflections. This is because John Quinn writes in a way that touches the heart and inspires the soul. His books reach into emotional, imaginative and inspirational territory, guiding the reader through these most important human domains. In *Gratias: A Little Book of Gratitude* he achieves that feat again.

There is nothing diminutive about this 'little' book of gratitude. As an 'anthology of memories, reflections, experiences, poems and prayers that express gratitude', its quotations are as extensive, potent, and salient in today's world as in the time in which many of them were written – right back to Cicero himself, born in 106 BC. For the core interior experiences of life do not change: the quest for love, acceptance, being and belonging; the mystery of blessings and belief; the journey through grief, mourning and yearning; everyday objects of interest and delight; a sense of place or the role of memory and meaning in our lives.

We develop a relationship with the world around us, with faith to sustain us, with nature to nurture us, with silence to soothe us, with others, with solitude and with ourselves. We recall what we have learnt from books, the refuge, the reassurance, the 'friendship' of the written word as it accompanies us through life. We recollect what we have learnt from our parents who support us, from teachers who encouraged us and from a sentence said to us that changed the course of our lives. We discover what we privilege in the present and can harvest from the past, and we value the psychological impact of everyday things. All these experiences are acknowledged in the quotations in this book, with its envoi both a tribute and dedication to Dr Mary Redmond's own anthology, *The Pink Ribbon Path.*

Just as the quotations selected for the book reveal something about the psychological disposition of the authors of those quotes, John's selection of quotations give insight into John Quinn himself. Through his compilation of this anthology we encounter him as a person, as a thinker and most especially as an educationalist, because in his own career, whether in the classroom or through media or as an RTÉ Radio producer, he is clearly a person with a passion to bestow on others the import of what he has spent a lifetime learning himself. Conveying information, igniting curiosity and inviting readers to consider perspectives are his hallmarks.

It is no accident, therefore, that the book is divided into sections which guide the reader through it. This makes it both educational and a delight to read. There are selections that are old, that are familiar, and some that are relatively new. There are nuggets of wisdom, expressions of emotions, poems, prose, proverbs and pronouncements. For young readers there is material that they may not have seen so far. For older readers there are encounters with former school texts committed to memory aeons ago – at the turn of a page 'forgotten' passages appear, bringing Proustian recollections of one's first encounters with them, while throughout the entire book there is the thematic backdrop of the importance of 'gratitude' in our psychological lives.

This gratitude theme is an important thread that runs through the pages because research is clear about the benefits to physical and mental health of fostering a grateful disposition. 'Practising gratitude' by recognising formally, at the beginning and end of each day, all that we are grateful for (however tiny) lays down neurological pathways in our brains that orient us towards having a positive disposition and beneficial recognition of the good things in our lives – even when we are going through bleak times. This process of recognising, enumerating, appreciating and articulating that for which we can be grateful, however initially inconsequential it may seem to be, has powerful psychotherapeutic effects.

Gratitude is deep recognition and appreciation. In simple psychological terms, gratitude is good for us. Indeed, the gift for which we should be most grateful is gratitude itself, because the more we express it, the more we experience it. It grows exponentially, extends out to others and acts as a powerful antidote to that which is crass, crude or cruel in the world. We need time out from trauma. Going into the psychological spaces that the quotations in this book provide cannot but ignite positive affirmations rather than negative attitudes in us.

But why would someone write yet another book about gratitude when shelves in bookshops groan with tomes of psychological research on how to think positively, live appreciatively, act decisively, multitask effectively and achieve spectacularly throughout life? Why, when there are online resources, mental fitness apps and maps, guides to wellness, well-being, emotional stability, cognitive care and rude good health, would a little ontological anthology have purchase or meaning in the world today? Perhaps because despite all the self-help aids available to us, we live in a world where the primary mental health problems are anxiety and depression; where young and older people are expressing angst, agitation, alienation and inability to cope with the overwhelming onslaught and vicarious trauma of daily negative news loops into our lives. The simplicity of this book is an antidote to that.

Psychology at its most efficacious is usually kind, compassionate, careful uncomplicated common sense. Sometimes we need simple solutions to complex problems – the inspiration of an apt word and the realisation that we are not alone in our emotions and our plight. There are many apposite reminders in this book of the thread that binds us all in our humanity. This is why I say, unashamedly, that you should acquire this 'therapeutic' anthology. Buy it, read it, open it each day and night, dip into it, skim through it, study it, peruse it, mark what touches your heart, give a copy to those you love and inscribe it with your gratitude for their presence in your life.

Dr Marie Murray
Clinical Psychologist and Author

Introduction

This little book is an anthology of memories, reflections, experiences, poems and prayers that express gratitude for many facets of life – the world about us, a loving God, everyday things, love, books, silence, faith, our own place, parents, mentors, health and healing.

It is dedicated to the memory of Dr Mary Redmond, a brilliant lawyer, academic and founder of a number of charities, including the Irish Hospice Foundation and The Wheel. One of the firmest tenets of her life and faith was gratitude for the graces and blessings we receive. She is, thus, in part the inspiration for this book, which I hope will engage the reader in reflection and in the words of Patrick Kavanagh:

So be reposed and praise, praise, praise
The way it happened and the way it is.

Being Thankful for …

The World About Us

If I were president, I would use my inaugural speech to challenge everyone to be thankful every time the sun rises and to show gratitude for all that it does for us.

Erling Kagge

———

When despair for the world grows in me
and I wake in the night at the least sound
in fear of what my life and my children's lives may be,
I go and lie down where the wood drake
rests in his beauty on the water, and the great
  heron feeds.
I come into the peace of wild things …
I rest in the grace of the world, and am free.

Wendell Berry

Some people, in order to discover God, read books. But there is a great book: the very nature of created things. Look above you. Look below you. Note it. Read it. God, whom you want to discover, never wrote that book with ink. Instead he set before your eyes the things he had made. Can you ask for a louder voice than that? Why, heaven and earth shout to you: 'God made me!'

St Augustine

———

... nature is never spent;
There lives the dearest freshness deep down things.

Gerard Manley Hopkins

Cogar
Bí séimh
Glac go fial le hiontas
Agus le haoibhness na cruinne.

A word –
Be gentle
And generously embrace the wonder
And the beauty of the universe.

Inscription on a bench in Shanganagh
Cemetery, Co. Dublin

I think that I shall never see
A poem lovely as a tree.

A tree whose hungry mouth is prest
Against the earth's sweet flowing breast;

A tree that looks at God all day,
And lifts her leafy arms to pray;

A tree that may in summer wear
A nest of robins in her hair;

Upon whose bosom snow has lain;
Who intimately lives with rain.

Poems are made by fools like me,
But only God can make a tree.

Joyce Kilmer

When I came home from McGill University I asked my father to show me our land. I had a map with me. He took it and ripped it up. 'You are thinking like a white man,' he said. 'Just walk the land with me the way your forefathers did. We have names for everything. I will show you where I saw my first moose, where the fish spawn, where the caribou calve, where the beavers dam the river.' This was a real learning curve for me, understanding how life depended on our living in harmony with nature.

Matthew Coon Come

The kiss of the sun for pardon,
The song of the birds for mirth,
One is nearer God's heart in a garden
Than anywhere else on earth.

Dorothy Frances Gurney

Glory be to God for dappled things –
For skies of couple-colour as a brinded cow;
For rose-moles all in stipple upon trout that swim;
Fresh-firecoal chestnut-falls; finches' wings;
Landscape plotted and pieced – fold, fallow, and
    plough;
And all trades, their gear and tackle and trim.

Gerard Manley Hopkins

A soft day, thank God!
A wind from the south
With a honeyed mouth;
A scent of drenching leaves,
Briar and beech and lime,
White elder-flower and thyme
And the soaking grass smells sweet,
Crushed by my two bare feet,

While the rain drips,
Drips, drips, drips from the eaves.

Winifred M. Letts

What would the world be, once bereft
Of wet and of wildness? Let them be left,
O let them be left, wildness and wet;
Long live the weeds and the wilderness yet.

Gerard Manley Hopkins

Being Thankful for …

A Loving God

Always be thankful. Let the message of Christ, in all its richness, find a home with you. Teach each other and advise each other in all wisdom. With gratitude in your hearts, sing psalms and hymns and inspired songs to God; and never say or do anything except in the name of the Lord Jesus, giving thanks to God the Father through him.

Colossians 3:15–17

———

In all thy ways acknowledge him, and he shall direct thy path.

Proverbs 3:6

Thank you, Lord, for being with us here today. Thank you, Lord, for sharing our sorrows. Thank you, Lord, for giving us hope. Thank you, Lord, for your great mercy. Thank you, Lord, because you wanted to be like one of us. Thank you, Lord, because you keep ever close to us, even when we carry our crosses. Thank you, Lord, for giving us hope. Lord, may no one rob us of hope! Thank you, Lord, because in the darkest moment of your own life, on the cross, you thought of us and you left us a mother, your mother. Thank you, Lord, for not leaving us orphans!

Pope Francis

I ask myself the question who is my neighbour and the answer I get is that my neighbour is not just my Protestant neighbour nor is it just my Catholic neighbour. I must include my terrorist neighbour if I believe what I am trying to say. It is true to say that Christ died for them too, and they are the children of God just as I am, and they must repent if they are going to get God's forgiveness, just as I must. That is why I like these words of John Greenleaf Whittier:

Follow with reverent steps the great example
Of him whose holy work was 'doing good':
So shall the wide earth seem our Father's
    temple,
Each loving life a psalm of gratitude.
Then shall all shackles fall; the stormy clangour
of wild war music o'er the earth shall cease;
Love shall tread out the baleful fire of anger
And in its ashes plant the tree of peace!
Gordon Wilson

My soul glorifies the Lord,
    my spirit rejoices in God my saviour.
He looks on his servant in her lowliness;
    Henceforth all generations will call me blessed.
The Almighty works marvels for me.
Holy his name!
His mercy is from age to age,
    On those who fear him.
He puts forth his arm in strength
    and scatters the proud hearted.
He casts the mighty from their thrones
    And raises the lowly.
He fills the starving with good things,
    sends the rich away empty.
He protects Israel, his servant,
    remembering his mercy,
    the mercy promised to our fathers,
    to Abraham and his sons for ever.

Mary, Mother of Jesus

When I met Gordon [Wilson] we were both compatible in terms of faith. We both had a strong faith. We were both Methodists. I wasn't aware so much of the hymns of John and Charles Wesley, but Gordon introduced me to so many of them. They are so wonderfully written and are so much part of my life. I love singing them – 'Love Divine, All Loves Excelling', 'Oh For a Thousand Tongues to Sing', 'A Charge to Keep I Have':

> A charge to keep I have
> A God to glorify
> A never-dying soul to save
> And fit it for the sky.

They are part of my prayer-life, of how I express my belief. A favourite of Gordon's was 'Jesus, Lover of My Soul':

> Other refuge have I none,
> Hangs my helpless soul on thee;
> Leave, ah leave me not alone,
> Still support and comfort me.

All my trust on thee is stayed,
All my help from thee I bring;
Cover my defenceless head
With the shadow of thy wing.

Joan Wilson

O give thanks to the Lord for he is good,
for his love endures for ever.
Give thanks to the God of gods,
for his love endures for ever;
who alone has wrought marvellous works,
for his love endures for ever;
whose wisdom it was made the skies,
for his love endures for ever;
who fixed the earth firmly on the seas,
for his love endures for ever.
It was he who made the great lights,
for his love endures for ever;
the sun to rule in the day
for his love endures for ever;

the moon and the stars in the night,
for his love endures for ever.

Psalm 135

I see his blood upon the rose
And in the stars, the glory of his eyes,
His body gleams amid eternal snows,
His tears fall from the skies.

I see his face in every flower;
The thunder and the singing of the birds
Are but his voice – and carven by his power
Rocks are his written words.

All pathways by his feet are worn,
His strong heart stirs the ever-beating sea,
His crown of thorns is twined with every thorn,
His cross is every tree.

Joseph Mary Plunkett

Being Thankful for ...

Books

'Oh, it's only a novel!' … only some work in which the greatest powers of the mind are displayed, in which the most thorough knowledge of human nature, the happiest delineations of its varieties … are conveyed to the world in the best-chosen language.

Jane Austen

A book is a personal experience between reader and author – an actual relationship. These 'friendships' – as I call them – have been part of my life and have been all the more delightful when unexpected. The person who opens a book acquires wings, and the better that book, the higher he flies. He does not travel alone. The writer bears him company and together they go hand in hand. And that is the purpose of – and the justification for – not only reading but for writing as well. To fly, not alone, but in companionship.

Hugh Leonard

My childhood was a solitary one that would have been a lonely one but for the company of my books and book friends. My clothes were all either hand-me-downs or home-made and how I empathised with Anne Shirley of *Anne of Green Gables* when she proclaimed, 'It's ever so much easier to be good if your clothes are fashionable.' Our family was small, but I lost myself in the bustle and warmth of the March family of *Little Women*. In truth I was probably much more like silly priggish Amy but fancied myself as Jo, as she climbed into the attic to munch apples and cry over some heroine in her book. I even took to saying 'Christopher Columbus' – the boldest utterance from Jo's mouth – and I wept bitter tears when she refused Laurie the boy next door. I read it so often that I'm almost convinced I could recite it by heart.

Patricia Donlon

A book is a private friend, speaking to us alone, telling us whatever we long to know. Every book makes its reader a welcome and honoured guest, free from all harm in the wildest and strangest places in the world. A book can dissolve the walls of the dullest room in the dullest town and no one seeing you sitting there can have any idea how far you have escaped.

Naomi Lewis

As a secondary school student I spent any pocket money I had on books in a secondhand bookstore in Belfast. I am afraid this became almost compulsive and I still find it hard to resist going into a bookshop. I have always felt that even just owning books is to some extent educative. There is a certain satisfaction in being familiar with a wider world of ideas. I have always found it stimulating.

Cardinal Cahal Daly

There were no books in our house, but I discovered them in the house of friends of my father, a family called Moroney. Father and son had a farm that they never looked after, but they gathered apples and sold them for a half-crown a bucketful. I remember being sent to buy apples and falling into conversation with the old man about books. When I was about eleven he gave me the run of his excellent nineteenth-century library. For about eight or nine years, I would come every fortnight, returning five or six books in my oil-cloth shopping bag and taking five or six more away.

I read every Zane Grey book in the library – thirty or forty novels. Somebody in that house was fascinated by the Rocky Mountains, so there was an endless amount of books about them, with all sorts of adventure stories. Then there were Scott and Dickens and Shakespeare. I don't think I differentiated between Zane Grey and Dickens. I just read for pleasure.

John McGahern

A book is a present you can open again and again.

Anonymous

———

Books, books, books!
I had found the secret of a garret-room.
Piled high with cases in my father's name;
Piled high, packed large, – where, creeping in and
    out
Among the giant fossils of my past,
Like some small nimble mouse between the ribs
Of a mastodon, I nibbled here and there
At this or that box, pulling through the gap,
In heats of terror, haste, victorious joy,
The first book first. And how I felt it beat
Under my pillow, in the morning's dark,
An hour before the sun would let me read!
My books!

Elizabeth Barrett Browning

Being Thankful for ...

The Gift of Love

For thy sweet love remembered such wealth
    brings
That then I scorn to change my state with kings.
                                    William Shakespeare

———

Love you. Miss you. Above all, above all, thank
you. Thank you for walking into my life thirty-
six years ago – and staying in it, especially when,
occasionally, you must have been tempted to walk
out of it! We had our highs and lows but in the
general mystery of life, we did alright … Of all the
throat-swab joints in all the world, you had to walk
into mine, swish that black leather coat and flash
that smile … *Deo Gratias.*

                                        John Quinn

The kingdom of God is about love. It's not the Church. It's not mystical experience. It's strong love and it has no distinctions, encompassing the entirety of humanity – Catholic, Buddhist, Hindu, Muslim, married, single, gay, straight. The message of Christianity is forgiveness and love. What is the point of anger and resentment towards others? Of course there is mystery. If there wasn't I would be equating myself with God.

Mary Redmond

I have been blessed with love. Erich Fromm says, 'Love is the only sane and satisfactory answer to the problem of existence.' So many people have a life without love. I am fortunate to be doing what I love surrounded by those I love.

Charles Handy

The highest tribute to the dead is not grief, but gratitude.

Thornton Wilder

———

I fell in love, just after the war, with Rupert who had been a bomber pilot and came to live in our village. He had this ramshackle ancient car and we drove all around the countryside at frightening speeds. We had a wonderful two years until it all came to an end. My family were dead set against our romance. Rupert was awaiting a divorce. He went away and subsequently remarried. But if I had to choose one memory from my life, it would be of a lovely summer afternoon with Rupert. The cuckoo was calling, the heavily scented elder trees were in flower. We didn't do anything but sit on the river bank, hold hands and talk. Rupert caught a tiny frog and released it again. There was something about that afternoon that was absolutely magic. I never experienced anything like it before or since.

Rosemary Sutcliff

Grief for another is the ultimate marker of the love of that other. It anoints with remembrance. It embraces with regret. It enfolds the person who was loved in loving recollection.

Marie Murray

… love that's proved by steady gazing
Not at each other but in the same direction.

Seamus Heaney

I met Joan at college. All the happiness of the rest of my life goes back to that period, meeting and falling in love at that time. Ours has been a very interactive marriage in which everything we have done we have done together. I have been constantly under challenge from her in the positions I have taken up – everything has to be argued out. Or if I take a wrong turning in some way, I am told so very quickly.

Garret FitzGerald

If life for me hath joy or light,
'Tis all from thee,
My thoughts by day, my dreams by night,
Are but of thee, of only thee.

Thomas Moore

———

Real love says 'Forever'. Love will always reach out toward the eternal. Love comes from that place within us where death cannot enter. Love does not accept the limits of hours, days, weeks, months or centuries. Love is not willing to be imprisoned by time.

Henri Nouwen

———

Say not in grief that he is no more but
in thankfulness that he was.

Hebrew Proverb

Before I met Richard, I was what could be called a routine Catholic. Richard brought my faith alive, made me examine it and commit myself to it. It was really a kind of conversion. Our love for each other deepened our rootedness in God. The great spiritual bond between us helped me cope with his loss after a year's marriage.

Mary O'Hara

Now winter's marching round Drumard
We'll log up stoves against the coming cold
Much to live for, still more to remember
And never, ever talk of growing old.
Light can catch the glory in November
Of summers past and though God gives no sign
When love is all there is no final line.

Eugene McCabe

She was the beat of my heart for thirty years. She was the music heard faintly at the edge of sound.

Raymond Carver

———

Your book [*Letters to Olive*] gripped and moved me. The best form of giving is thanksgiving. Your book is a grammar of gratitude for Olive.

Mary Redmond

A person should always offer a prayer of graciousness for the love that has awakened in them. When you feel love for your beloved and his or her love for you, now and again you should offer the warmth of your love as a blessing for those who are damaged or unloved. Send that love out into the world to people who are desperate; to those who are starving; to those who are trapped in prison, in hospitals and all the brutal terrains of bleak and tormented lives. When you send that love out from the bountifulness of your own love, it reaches other people. This love is the deepest power of prayer.

John O'Donohue

Being Thankful for ...

A Gifted Teacher

At times our light goes out and is rekindled by a spark from another person. Each of us has cause to think with deep gratitude of those who have lighted the flame within us.

Albert Schweitzer

———

Unquestionably, the biggest influence in my life was Fr Vincent Kennedy; now dead, God rest his soul. Looking back, I have met many, many eminent people, but he was really one of the most sophisticated men I ever met. He was a very stylish man. He was small and dapper and everything he did was very graceful. He had a rather lovely room in St Patrick's College, with a Bechstein piano and a very nice library. He used to produce operas. I was a boy soprano. My first appearance on the stage was in *The Yeomen of the Guard*. I had an extraordinarily powerful boy soprano voice, something I inherited from my father. When my voice broke, we used to go up to Fr Vincent's room and he would play us a wide variety of music. He also gave us classes in school in general music education and the history of music. He would demonstrate the difference in structure between the work of Beethoven and Chopin, for example, and the development of the piano as an instrument. This was very, very fascinating and unusual for a secondary school. We would listen to the Proms on BBC in his room and follow it with the score. He had a wonderful range as a classical pianist. He could play the Grieg concerto from memory and he had hundreds of scores as well.

We were the chosen few – just three or four of us – like Jean Brodie's crème de la crème. We would knock on his door after night prayer and if he was in a good mood he would let us in. We would have coffee and talk and he would play the piano.

TP McKenna

I had the extraordinary fortune of having a marvellous holistic primary teacher in a two-teacher school in Newmarket-on-Fergus, a man by the name of William Clune.

He defeated time because he was going back as well as forward. He knew the names of plants and bushes in Latin and Irish and English and, on sunny days, he used to take the whole school to the top of a hill to show them the history of the local area. He had an integrated approach to everything before that word was invented. He was a man with an extraordinary sense of history in his own life too, because his brother was Conor Clune, the National Volunteer who had been shot just before the founding of the state.

He was a man who loved the wonder of children and he had some extraordinary ideas, which I am sure couldn't be proved. He had an idea, for example, that if you tried hard enough and used your concentration, you could go back through not only your own memory but other people's memories to remember an Irish work. He was a Jungian. Everything that I was later to encounter about Jung and consciousness, he was in fact practising in his own way in the schoolyard. There was not one person who came into his schoolyard from any background, with shoes or without, who wasn't respected as a carrier of wonderment. It was the central value of his pedagogic technique.

Michael D. Higgins

In the tech I met an extraordinary teacher, Sean Cleary. He had worked in England for Vickers and elsewhere, so he could give you a vision of what engineering and metalwork could be like. He also had a deep sense of quality of workmanship and he would sometimes hold up a piece of material and say, 'Isn't that beautiful, just surface finished?' The culture that was transmitted just by doing that was very powerful. I told him I was very keen to design and build a steam engine and he was a good enough facilitator and teacher to say, 'Well, alright, let's try and do it.' The only machine tool we had was a lathe and with him I designed and built a double-acting steam engine which I have to this day. It was a very, very formative experience. We needed close-grain cast iron for the cylinders and there was simply none in Tuam. Now if I was going to be a good civil servant I would have learned at that stage that you write a report about the material you want, you then write saying there is none available and you conclude that the project can't be done. But we heard that there was an old sawmill with an abandoned flywheel and we knew that a flywheel has to stand high centrifugal forces, so it would have been made from good close-grain cast iron. So we went and cut a huge chunk of cast iron out of it, divided it up into pieces and made a marvellous steam engine.

Mike Cooley

I went to a second level school in Tarbert that was run by an amazing woman. Her name was Jane Agnes McKenna and she had two teachers, Pat and Alice Carey. She taught languages and some kind of commerce, but her emphasis was on words and on trying to tell the truth. She used to get very angry about telling lies and it was the only thing she would slap you for. Her love of literature was genuine and profound. She would get us all to say speeches from Shakespeare. It was great to hear the lads reciting *Macbeth*, *Hamlet* and *Othello* in north Kerry accents. The best way to experience words is to commit them to memory. As you walk along the street or sit down in pubs and talk to friends, you can allow your mind to be visited by words that you learned many years ago. Miss McKenna, as we used to call her, handed us this ability to be haunted, to leave our hearts and minds open to Shakespeare, to Latin, to French and to Irish. We had to write a lot at the weekend and then we would have to stand up in class and read it out, and read out other people's writing as well. It was a life of expression. Later when I suffered from moments of depression, I learned that expression is the best way to heal depression and that it is necessary at every level to utter yourself.

Brendan Kennelly

Not everything that can be counted counts, and not everything that counts can be counted.

Albert Einstein

Being Thankful for …

Silence, Solitude – and Doing Nothing

I love silence. I have a beautiful quotation from the Philokalia [Eastern Orthodox text]: 'I see that you too have been wounded by the arrow of the love of silence.' I don't think my love of silence is necessarily due to my time in the monastery. It's innate in me. There is a silence which is part of music, threading its way through – as John Montague put it – 'The delicate dance of silence.'

I loved the silences of Africa. I love 'nothing', when there is no noise around. Just to sit and be.

Mary O'Hara

Alone in my small cell
Peace for company
Before meeting with death.

A very cold bed
Fearful, like the sleep
Of a doomed man.

Sleep, short and restless,
Invocations
Frequent and early.

Let this shelter me
These holy walls
A spot beautiful and sacred
And I there alone.

Eighth-Century Monk

College was a wonderful period in my life. It was a very relaxed existence. The war years were a very sheltered period for us. There was no question of working in the summer holidays. There was no work to be done anyway. We learned to do nothing for three months on end, which I think is a marvellous thing to have experienced for some period of your life. I have never regretted my idleness for those summers.

Garret FitzGerald

Silence is a great act of expression. Miss McKenna [our teacher] taught us to be silent every evening. I have kept that habit, particularly in the morning when I wake up and my mind is full of dreams. I can sit there and write without trying to explain and, above all, without trying to analyse the dreams that have visited me during the night.

Brendan Kennelly

Today's world is not conducive to reflection. Everybody is in a rush but I always try to find the time and space to reflect. I have a simple prayer I say every morning: 'Dear God, this is the day you have made and I am glad to be part of it.' I go on to seek the guidance of the Spirit for what we do.

Alice Leahy

Nothing in the world resembles God
as much as silence.

Meister Eckhart

What did I do on my Auntie Nan's farm?

I did nothing. I sat by a well and saw a spider race with delicate legs across the cold water from out of his cavern. I saw a line of cows pass along a road, their udders dripping into the dust. I went with Uncle Tom, each of us seated on a shaft of the donkey cart jolting out to his bits of fields in the Commons near Lough Doohyle, taking with us for the day a bottle of cold tea and great slices of wheel cakes cooked in a bastable, plastered with country butter and cheap jam. While, all day, he went slowly up and down the ridges on one knee thinning his turnips, I wandered. I saw a row of twenty poplars whispering to the wind. I picked and chewed the seeds of the pink mallow. I saw how the branch of a thorn tree in the armpit of the alder had worn itself and its lover smooth from squeakily rubbing against it for forty years. I saw an old ruined castle and a Big House with the iron gates hanging crookedly from its carved pillars. And all the time away across the saucer of the lake there was the distant church spire of Rathkeale, like a finger of silence rising from an absolutely level horizon.

You see? Nothing! A fairy tale, a child's memory, a cradle song, crumbs in a pocket, dust, a seed. I lay on my back among lone fields and wondered whether the cloudy sky was moving or stopped. Childhood, boyhood, nostalgia, tears. Things no traveller would notice or want to notice but things from which a boy of this region would never get free, things wrapping cataracts of love about his eyes, knotting tendrils of love about his heart.

Seán O'Faoláin

Animals carry huge witness to the silence of time and depth of nature. Meister Eckhart said that nothing in the universe resembles God so much as silence. To come into silence is to come into the presence of the divine – that silence of intimacy where no word is needed, where a word might even be a fracture. One of the great healing functions of landscape is that it is the custodian of a great unclaimed silence that urbanised postmodern society has not raided yet. This landscape [Mamean Mountain], living in a mode of silence, is wrapped in seamless prayer.

John O'Donohue

This [my grandfather's farm] is a very quiet place, full of wonderful silence. As a child when I came here I was full of loneliness and lostness. We're looking across at what used to be a poppy field. I melt into that field when I think of it. I would walk into the middle of it as a child and sit down in this sea of red. I was a tiny child, so the poppies enveloped me in a glistening lime green forest of stalks ... Listen to that apparent silence! There's a dog barking, probably miles away. The crows are shifting in the trees. My paintings come out of silence. There is a moment when painting is no longer an act of doing or making but of receiving. I came up here and still do, for these 'silent' places – that kind of silence, where you can hear a fly hopping from one leaf to another, a silence that carried sounds from out of my existence into it. This is where my painting comes from.

Paddy Graham

The essence of all beautiful art, of all art,
is gratitude.

Friedrich Nietzsche

———

Silence is a very scarce commodity in modern life. It's almost as if we are afraid of it. There's a tendency to fill silent spaces with music and noise. Silence removes the barriers to our internal reality. Are we nervous of being alone with ourselves? But being alone with ourselves is very calming. If I sit in my garden and watch and listen to the birds or watch the moon in the night sky, it is something magical. Yet this is only what is visible to us, and beyond that there is great wonder that we are not privy to. God is the conduit of our own inner goodness.

Alice Taylor

Being Thankful for ...

Parents

My father had beautiful copperplate handwriting and was a highly intelligent man. A lot of people in the district used to come to him to write their letters for them, or to write letters to the local authority. So, from a very early age – as we didn't have a very big house – I was conscious of people and their problems. We had two bedrooms, one living room and a parlour, and people would queue up waiting for my father as he sat writing at the table. He was very committed to helping people solve their problems, because he had a very good knowledge of the whole system.

Without the dedication and self-sacrifice of my mother, I don't think I would have gotten anywhere in life. She was totally committed to rearing us in the best possible way, with very, very limited resources, and when I look back I just don't know how she did it. I am absolutely convinced that the major influence on any life is the parents and that this takes place in the early years of a child. Even though usually buried in the subconscious, these are the forces that create you and make you what you are and give you your attitude to life.

John Hume

———

Let us be thankful to the people who make us happy; they are the charming gardeners who make our souls blossom.

Marcel Proust

God made my mother on an April day,
From sorrow and the mist along the sea,
Lost birds' and wanderers' songs and ocean spray,
And the moon loved her wandering jealously.

Beside the ocean's din she combed her hair,
Singing the nocturne of the passing ships,
Before her earthly lover found her there
And kissed away the music from her lips.

She came unto the hills and saw the change
That brings the swallow and the geese in turns.
But there was not a grief she deemed strange,
For there is that in her which always mourns.

Kind heart she has for all on hill or wave
Whose hopes grew wings like ants to fly away.
I bless the God who such a mother gave
This poor bird-hearted singer of a day.

Francis Ledwidge

To encourage creativity in her children, my mother took the unusual step of painting one of the kitchen walls black and providing us with a box of coloured chalks. She felt that – because children cannot scale things down – they should not be made to contain their idea of a person or a flower to a page in a notebook; they should draw something as they see it – life-size or even larger. So we used to spend our days drawing on the black wall. This had a number of advantages. As far as my mother was concerned, it meant that we were very quiet and that she could keep an eye on us. For our part, it encouraged self-expression and we were given prizes for the best drawing. We never realised, of course, that my mother gave the prizes exactly in rota.

My mother was in many ways a most unconventional woman. When my father was away on business she would keep us home from school for two or three days at a time, switch off the radio and turn the clock to the wall. She would write and we children would undertake curious and elaborate – if often useless – pieces of housework, like washing rugs in a tin bath or making toffee at the kitchen table. We had a glorious time. We went to the pictures in the evening and extended the fantasy by always trying to eat whatever the people ate in the pictures.

I realise now that this was my mother's silent protest against the extremely conventional lives that women lived then. She dressed up to go to the shops as other women did – she put on her high heels, pearls and gloves to go down to the shop for a bag of potatoes! She obviously hated all this, so in the privacy of her own house – when there was nobody around to approve or disapprove – she lived as she wished to live.

Clare Boylan

My mother was a woman of great strength and forcefulness, like many, many women of her generation. Her religious faith, her identification with the suffering Mother of Christ, was the way in which she survived the biological penalty of child after child. There were nine of us inside of about twelve years. Women in those days were cornered in childbearing, in exhaustion, in a kind of resentment of their position, both sexually and in every other way. Hence, their intense devotion to the Blessed Virgin Mary, their devotion to the Rosary, that triumphant cry that you used to hear in country churches when women were answering the prayers. Within the realm of prayer there was a place for resistance; it provided a bracing other value that could be set against the penalties of the lived life. My mother had a very strong faith and it wasn't just a matter of religiosity or piety, it was a matter of fierce spiritual commitment. I think that I identified with that and I took it in too. I suppose that is always something Oedipal in the boy growing up with the Mammy, but this was a process of osmosis from her spirit.

Seamus Heaney

When all the others were away at Mass
I was all hers as we peeled potatoes.
They broke the silence, let fall one by one
Like solder weeping off the soldering iron:
Cold comforts set between us, things to share
Gleaming in a bucket of clean water.
And again let fall. Little pleasant splashes
From each other's work would bring us to our senses.

So while the parish priest at her bedside
Went hammer and tongs at the prayers for the dying
And some were responding and some crying
I remembered her head bent towards my head,
Her breath in mine, our fluent dipping knives –
Never closer the whole rest of our lives.

Seamus Heaney

Grandma [Lady Gregory] was the centre of our lives here in Coole, where we were born and bred. She wasn't just Grandma – she was really our mother. She could be quite a disciplinarian, but for her the important things were 'always be on time' and 'manners maketh man'. She had incredible friendliness. Class or creed meant nothing to her. If, in the middle of a day's work, someone came to the door looking for apples or sticks, it didn't matter to her. She would come down and have a chat. The extraordinary thing was while we were having this wonderful life here, she was writing, running the Abbey [Theatre], going up and down to Dublin … but she would always have time for us. She might be in the middle of writing a play when we would rush in to tell her of a bird's nest we had found. She would drop everything at once to hear our story.

She was our teacher – and a slightly easy-going one too. She taught us our tables and simple arithmetic, some French also, but her pronunciation was appalling. We had to read a chapter of the Bible to her every morning. She would read to us every evening, anything from *Brer Rabbit* to James Fenimore Cooper. *Swiss Family Robinson* was our favourite book. We used to act it out, pretending our pony was an ostrich on a desert island.

When you look at photographs of Grandma, she looks like Queen Victoria – all in black – but she actually had a great sense of humour. She was never a prude. We had a general knowledge book full of questions like, 'Why in public places does water at drinking troughs always come out of the mouth of a lion?' Grandma said, 'Well, it would look awful coming out of the other end!' And then exploded into laughter. She just couldn't stop. I can still see her with her hankie up to her eyes, the tears streaming down her cheeks.

Anne & Catherine Gregory

Being Thankful for …

Everyday Things

This is a wonderful day. I've never seen
this one before.

Maya Angelou

———

I want to talk to thee of little things
So fond, so frail, so foolish that one clings
To keep them ours – who could but understand
A joy in speaking them, thus hand in hand.

Beside the fire; our joys, our hope, our fears,
Our secret laughter, our unchidden tears;
Each day old dreams come back with beating
    wings,
I want to speak of these forgotten things.

Dora Sigerson Shorter

The philosopher Meister Eckhart once said, 'If the only prayer you say in your life is "Thank you", that would be enough.' I feel it is so important to give thanks to the Lord for all that we are, all that we have, all that we hope to be. So last thing at night, I reflect on five things to be thankful for – simple things like a phone call from one of my children, a pleasant meal, a book or music I enjoyed, sunshine, a page or two of writing. There is never a shortage of subjects.

John Quinn

It is a magical thing to be delighted. I try to be delighted about everything – the primroses, the nape of a baby's neck …

Maureen Potter

Grace Before Meals

Bless us o Lord, and these thy gifts, which of thy
bounty we are about to receive, through Christ
our Lord. Amen.

Grace After Meals

We give thee thanks, Almighty God, for all thy
benefits, through Christ our Lord. Amen.

The greatest poem in the English language is the
    Present Indicative tense of the verb 'to be':
I am, thou art,
He is, she is,
We are, you are,
They are.

Richard Burton

In this life we cannot do great things. We can only do small things – with great love.

Mother Teresa

I wake up each morning incredibly grateful for my life, for my good health and the health of my children and my husband, Steve, grateful for Steve's love and all the love in my life, grateful for just everything. I find that living with that attitude to life, every single day is a terrific stress-buster.

Miriam O'Callaghan

Cultivate the habit of being grateful for every good thing that comes to you and to give thanks continuously. And because all things have contributed to your advancement, you should include all things in your gratitude.

Ralph Waldo Emerson

I was walking down the pavement the other day. Outside a delicatessen there was a sandwich board with the heading 'Today's Special'. They hadn't filled in the bottom part. I was tempted to find a piece of chalk and fill it in with the words – 'So is every day!'

Roger McGough

———

The rose is without why
She blooms because she blooms
She does not care for herself
Asks not if she is seen …

Angelus Silesius

It was the garden of the golden apples,
A long garden between a railway and a road,
In the sow's rooting where the hen scratches
We dipped our fingers in the pockets of God.
In the thistly hedge old boots were flying sandals
By which we travelled through the childhood
    skies,
Old buckets rusty-holed with half-hung handles
Were drums to play when old men married wives.

The pole that lifted the clothes-line in the middle
Was the flag-pole on a prince's palace when
We looked at it through fingers crossed to riddle
In evening sunlight miracles for men.

Patrick Kavanagh

If you must look back, do so forgivingly.
If you must look forward, do so prayerfully.
However, the wisest thing you can do is be
present in the present, gratefully.

Maya Angelou

At every moment
There is a moment
To be seized.
So seize it
There and then!
For you know
That you will never have
That moment
Again.

John Quinn

———

Get down on your knees and give thanks that
you are still on your feet.
A saying beloved of my mother

I am surprised every morning when I awake to find the world intact. There is everywhere evidence of nature's optimism. The light is new. The rain sumptuously wet. When the sun shines we know that everything is possible. Every morning we are younger than we were the night before. Our duty and pleasure should be to delight in this youthfulness.

William Crozier

Help me to accept my everyday
just as it is,
the quirky pains and aches
all over,
tenderness in hands and feet.
This, my everyday
I lay before you as it is.

Help me to love my everyday,
every moment
where I can be 'all there' with you
and 'all here'

giving myself unreservedly to this oneness.
This, my everyday
I lay before you as it is.

Thank you for this everyday,
your healing touch
in every cell,
re-bodying me,
my presence to my deepest self.
This, my everyday
I lay before you as it is.

Mary Redmond

Being Thankful for …

The Gift of Faith

I am grateful now for the faith I have and the God I believe in. I don't think I was always grateful for everything I received, which was enormous. Gratitude is something you learn and it is the way of being which we are most at home in. That's what the Book of Psalms is all about – praise and gratitude. It's not really possible to praise and thank, unless you believe in God. When you do, that is the most appropriate and most satisfying stance you can take. I certainly am happy to take that stance and to create a life in a monastery where praise and thanks constitute the meaning and structure of our lives.

Mark Patrick Hederman

I am very comfortable with the sense of values that my faith encompasses. Saint Paul sums it up: 'And now faith, hope and love abide … and the greatest of these is love.' That is the core of the Christian idea. The core values are pointing towards some ultimate unification when all will be one. The Creed says it all, really: 'I believe in all things visible and invisible.' Great literature has always influenced me. *The Great Gatsby* has touched me at different stages of my life. I took the last sentence – 'So we beat on, boats against the current, borne back ceaselessly into the past' – as the epigraph for my book, *Going by Water*. It's a metaphor for the journey of life, I suppose.

Michael Coady

Happy indeed is the man
who follows not the counsel of the wicked;
nor lingers in the way of sinners
nor sits in the company of scorners,
but whose delight is the law of the Lord
and who ponders his law day and night.

He is like a tree that is planted
beside the flowing waters,
that yields its fruit in due season
and whose leaves shall never fade;
and all that he does shall prosper.

Psalm 1:1–3

There is an idea of 'faith' as something you go into church for, get down on your knees and grind your teeth until you 'believe' and then you go out to face the world. I think it's a different process: that of looking deeply into what is real and looking at people and their lives, seeing the mystery of where they came from and the extraordinary phenomenon that the human being is. People say to me, 'Why did Jesus come?' I'm here! You're here! Isn't that reason enough to start with? Consider that there are seven billion beings on this planet and you are one of them. This planet is a tiny speck going round a tiny star in a galaxy which is one of billions of galaxies in the universe. I am here now, a subjective consciousness looking out at reality. That's an amazing thing! Darwinism doesn't get to that level of understanding. The transcendent, the sacred and the holy are dismissed by many out of a desire not to be irrational. I have no problem with Darwin. He may explain everyone else but he doesn't explain me. As Giussani said, faith is knowledge.

John Waters

I look on faith as a journey of discovery. Faith implies doubt, there's no question about that. People who claim absolute certainty in faith are as bad as atheistic scientists who tell us there is no such thing as God. No serious scientist would make such a statement because they cannot prove it. It is equally true – and there will be religious people who won't like this – that we cannot prove the existence of God in a scientific way. I love the example of Abraham in the Old Testament: 'Abraham set out not knowing where he was going.' That is a powerful idea which should help other people who are struggling with faith, because that is the kind of journey that it is.

Gordon Linney

Of course I have had doubts and falterings in my faith life. Sometimes we wonder where is God in the midst of suffering. My sister had an aneurysm and is totally paralysed. I asked her husband and children if they ever despaired. They thought about it and said no, not really. Such amazing courage is hard to rationalise, but I suppose in times of trial we pray together in a lifeboat situation. There is a plaque outside my office which says, 'Bidden or not bidden, God is present.'

Sean Boylan

I think doubt accompanies faith. Every day we encounter doubts. I try to counteract them with acts of faith. I pray, 'Jesus, Son of God, have mercy on me.' Or I recall that wonderful quotation from the prophet Micah, 'There is only one thing Yahweh asks of you, only this – to love tenderly, to act justly and to walk humbly with your God.' That sums it all up for me. I am anchored in my belief and grateful. I came across another quotation: 'The best thing you can do for yourself ever, no matter what happens to you is to praise and thank God.' I am grateful for the gifts that have been showered on me, left, right and centre, and for the strength to cope with the not-so-good things.

Mary O'Hara

My faith is completely central to my life and my work. It informs and imbues every aspect of my life for the better. My work and my life are not separate. There can be a great temptation to allow work to take over your life. Laurence Freeman described meditation as the 'wind in the sail of your soul'. If I want to experience that wind, I will turn off my phones, close my files, avoid the emails and make space for what is important. In the evening, I look over the events of the day, assess my behaviour, how it affected people, how I related to them. The community and voluntary sector is a very important part of my life – finding what can be done for the underprivileged, the poor (not necessarily in monetary terms), the marginalised. Life is like a three-legged stool – the legs being work, community and family. I am still on the path of trying to grow my faith, which I value more than I can possibly put in words. Doubts still persist. I can't always quell negative aspects of my ego, which may tempt me to go in different directions. Gandhi once said, 'I have so much to do today, I am going to have to meditate for two hours rather than one.' So yes, there are crosswinds, but I don't feel without help.

Faith is a gift for which I am exceedingly grateful. I give thanks that for some reason or other I listened to that invitation to love. Nothing that I did myself made me deserve it. I am also grateful for some of the bad things that have happened to me, because out of them has come good. The most supremely bad thing that ever happened was Jesus on the cross, and look what came out of that! I am grateful for all the insights and experiences I have gained and, above all, for the great gift of faith. That gift is there for everyone.

Mary Redmond

Being Thankful for …

Our Own Place

In the fields and streets where you grew up, there you will always live and there you will die.

Cavafy

———

Ardboe, Co. Tyrone was a paradisiacal place to grow up in, and we were particularly isolated. You look around and you cannot see another house. On one side is the massive natural barrier that is Lough Neagh while on the other is a great man-made concrete barrier – the aerodrome, built in the 1940s. Lough Neagh was a huge dominating influence on all our lives. It is so vast, you could as well be looking out at the Irish Sea. Today, the sky is grey, pewter, oppressive, making the lough look like a vast shield of armour, but on the other days it can change mood entirely. The slap and the sough of the waves became so much part of us that we didn't hear it.

The aerodrome, which was inoperable a lot of the time because of mist and fog from the lake, was an extraordinary place, somewhat like a medieval patch of land. When I began to explore it, I developed my passion for natural life. I was moved by reading that Wordsworth said he had been 'sprung' into poetry by hearing a walnut fall. Wherever we grow up, we have all had the equivalent of Wordsworth's walnut – some secret childhood sound which, if we hear it again, will bring us back to where we were. The walnut in my life came when I saw the skylark rise from its nest and soar above me. No matter how high it climbs, you never lose sight of it. And then down from this tiny black speck comes this extraordinary song that falls like silvery blue shavings of sound all about you. Anything that is poetic in me was awakened by that sound, the song of the skylark.

Polly Devlin

The strand at Ringsend was our playground. It was there that we would re-enact the Tom Mix movies that we had seen earlier in the Assembly Rooms for twopence. We would pinch a few potatoes at home, dig cockles out of the strand, gather charcoal and light a fire, roast the potatoes and boil cockles in an old can. A royal feast! Afterwards we would play rounders or follow the fishermen who were catching salmon in the Liffey. If they caught any other fish, they threw it to us children and we would bring it home. I was very close to my grandfather, who was a carpenter. We would wander the beach collecting wood, from which he would model a ship for me.

James Plunkett

My grandfather's farm in Co. Westmeath was full of 'caves' – glades among the trees – which were secret places for me as a child for hiding and listening. I would climb into the trees and talk to them and to myself and look out at the world. The magical shadows and dappled light were a visual and sensual delight for me. Then I would come out into the open, a stunning, sculptural green as the sun lit up everything. This is cinema to me, like rolling a wonderful movie, a magical dreamlike world. This is a lived-in rolled-up landscape that folds in on itself like whipped cream. I am earthed to here. I belong to here. This is where I pray, not in words but in wonder about nature.

Paddy Graham

There would have been about seventy children in 'The Park' in North Dublin where I grew up. After school, everyone went out to play on the street or green. They would break up into small groups and play an amazing range of games – skipping, ball games, make-believe, beds, marbles, chasing or games of just pure devilment! It reminds me of a sentence from the bible: 'And the streets shall be filled with the sounds of boys and girls playing.'

We played simply for joy. We were never bored and games cost nothing. A piece of rope attached to a lamp post or strung between two gateposts and you could swing away to your heart's delight. Boys lifted the lid of the water hydrant and it became a mowl into which they pitched buttons or coins. A piece of chalk and an empty shoe-polish tin were all you needed for 'beds' or hopscotch. Just hopping up and down steps became the basis for another game. We used our environment …

Adults didn't pay (or didn't need to pay) the slightest attention to children's games. This was the only time children were totally without adult supervision. We made our own rules. There were

no prizes – just the joy of 'waiting your chance'
and maybe occasionally winning a game. When
you were 'out' that was it. You accepted that and
waited your chance again. We learned to socialise
and accept rules.

It was, of course, another era, another Dublin,
but for me it was paradise that is lost to today's
children.

Eilís Brady

We're standing now in the Fair Green in Carrick-on-Suir, Co. Tipperary. I grew up beside the green but wouldn't have realised then how ancient a space this was. It was the commonage of the town in the twelfth century. I can almost read the history of the last century about me. Behind me is the parish church of St Nicholas and attached to it is the Presentation Convent. The nuns came here in 1813 and gradually colonised almost the entire block. I played hurling in this green in my childhood. This was where circuses and carnivals came and, of course, where fairs were held. Father Mathew preached on temperance here. Daniel O'Connell held a monster meeting here and the local Temperance Band played 'God Save the Queen' to welcome him. Two hundred years ago, the Dorset Militia paraded here. All of these events find echo now in the empty space of the Fair Green.

Michael Coady

The Coal Quay was a great place for entertainment too. Wherever there was a crowd, fellows would come doing all kinds of acts. One fellow would turn himself into a monkey, twisting his legs over his arms and making a monkey shape. Another would lie on a bed of broken glass or nails. And there would be chancers like the fellow who had this magic stain remover. He would call a little boy from the audience, throw ink on his shirt and then rub away the ink with this block of blue stuff. My mother was delighted at this, bought the blue stuff, brought it home and threw ink over my brother's good Communion shirt. She began rubbing it with the 'magic' stuff and, of course, if she was rubbing it still, it wouldn't work. The shirt was destroyed. 'The devil hoist that fellow,' she cried. 'If I ever see him again, I'll reef him!' And, of course, she never did see him again.

Banjo Annie would come of a Saturday night and play songs like 'Two Little Girls in Blue'. Another fellow entertained us on a Saturday night with Shakespeare. He'd light candles and perform in one of the stalls. He'd do the Shakespeare all wrong but it was brilliant altogether! Sure where would you get entertainment like that for nothing?

It was all life here in the Coal Quay. To me, this was the real heart of old Cork – much more than Patrick Street. I loved coming here.

Eibhlís de Barra

Being Thankful for ...

Contentment

Clear days bring the mountains down to my
    door-step,
calm nights give the rivers their say,
the wind puts its hand to my shoulder some
    evenings,
and then I don't think,
I just leave what I'm doing and I go the soul's way.
John Moriarty

———

Joy is the simplest form of gratitude.

Karl Barth

I turn the lea-green down
Gaily now,
And paint the meadow brown
With my plough.

I dream with silvery gull
And brazen crow.
A thing that is beautiful
I may know.

Tranquillity walks with me
And no care.
O, the quiet ecstasy
Like a prayer.

I find a star-lovely art
In a dark sod.
Joy that is timeless! O heart
That knows God!

Patrick Kavanagh

The best of life is lived quietly, where nothing happens but our quiet journey through the day, where change is imperceptible and the precious life is everything.

John McGahern

I would maintain that thanks are the highest form of thought; and that gratitude is happiness doubled by wonder.

Gilbert Keith Chesterton

When I look into the well of my life, I am happy with the decisions I made. In the middle of all the ups and downs, twists and turns, I am happy that there was a constant search in me for God. And God gives all of what we need, in whatever measure we need. When I take time to question, it all makes sense to me. Things fit.

Phyllis Kilcoyne

Happy the man, whose wish and care
A few paternal acres bound,
Content to breathe his native air,
In his own ground.

Whose herds with milk, whose fields with bread,
Whose flocks supply him with attire,
Whose trees in summer yield him shade,
In winter fire.

Blest, who can unconcern'dly find
Hours, days, and years slide soft away,
In health of body, peace of mind,
Quiet by day,

Sound sleep by night; study and ease
Together mix'd; sweet recreation,
And innocence, which most does please,
With meditation.

Thus let me live, unseen, unknown;
Thus unlamented let me die;
Steal from the world, and not a stone
Tell where I lie.

Alexander Pope

Gratitude is an essential part of being present.
When you go deeply into the present, gratitude
arises spontaneously.

Eckhart Tolle

Joe farmed a few acres of what we call 'marginal land' in Ireland for more than fifty years. I was fortunate to have his friendship for a while and loved to walk with him through his realm, helping him clear *sceachs* [stunted hawthorn trees], taking cuttings for new hedgerows, mulching his fruit trees, or helping him collect small quantities of honey from his hives.

Every day Joe strolled through his land with his hands clasped behind his back, at peace with the silence and feeling no compulsion to chat. He seemed at ease and I felt wholly accepted in his company. He accepted whatever life threw at him and was grateful for all that was in his life at that moment. He emanated grace at all times. Joe was simply himself.

He began farming in a natural way many years before and was considered an eccentric within his local farming community. He never had much, but he always seemed happy with his lot in life. I asked him about it one day, but his reply confused me at the time: 'Sure what else would I need?'

I remember one particular conversation with Joe. It was a lazy summer day and we were sitting on an old stone wall beside a grassy meadow. I thought to ask Joe if he believed in God. He smiled to himself and then he talked a little about God and religion.

Eventually Joe leaned over, plucked a stalk of flowering grass and held it up for me to examine. I will never forget what he said because it struck me like a hammer with its clear and simple truth. 'Mary,' he said, while contemplating the flower for a moment, 'this is God.'

Mary Reynolds

Being Thankful for ...

The Gift of Memory

Nothing is ever really lost, or can be lost,
No birth, identity, form – no object of the world.
Nor life, nor force, nor any visible thing;
Appearance must not foil, nor shifted sphere
    confuse thy brain.
Ample are time and space – ample the fields of
    Nature.
The body, sluggish, aged, cold – the embers left
    from earlier fires,
The light in the eye grown dim, shall duly flame
    again …

Walt Whitman

Memory gives us roses in December.
Brendan Kennelly

———

Great is the power of memory, exceedingly great,
O my God, a spreading limitless room within me.
Who can reach its uttermost depth? Yet it is a
faculty of soul and belongs to my nature. In fact I
cannot totally grasp all that I am.

St Augustine

———

Memory is a way of comprehending.
Seamus Heaney

Aural sound and sound sense were born for me on those musky eiderdown days, behind the top window of my grandmother's house on Main Street. Aural sound was to be my first introduction to theatre, to the arts and to the unbounding possibilities of radio and writing and teaching. It was my beginning and my understating of how my place spoke to me. It spoke to me through the music and melody and patterns and inflections and phraseology and emphasis and pitch and lift and fall of the word music of the human voice.

It is my sound memory that has held onto every memory of my past. It is the one I carry with me everywhere. My first 'on the ear' experiences. And it has fuelled and fired and given voice to all that I have attempted across the arts and teaching and politics.

I have never left that bedroom.

Marie-Louise O'Donnell

Memory is our second chance at happiness.

Pegg Monahan

India was quite an exotic place to grow up in at that time [Milligan was born in Ahmednagar, India in 1918]. The sights, the sounds, the scents ... I remember the lines of marching regiments – Sikhs, Gurkhas, etc. – in their bright turbaned uniforms, the beating of the leopard-skin drums, the blare of silver bugles from the Ulster and Connaught Rifles. How lucky I was to see it all. We travelled a lot because some bureaucrat in London would justify his existence by moving regiments hither and thither. Bombay, Calcutta, Karachi – on the Peninsular Railway – often four or five-day journeys. I remember the train pulling into some remote station at night and the vendors would call out, offering Biddy cigarettes, hot milk, oranges and bananas. Then the great hiss of steam as we moved off, with the kitehawks screaming overhead. When we passed over a great river gorge the sound changed dramatically – ticket-a-tick, ticket-a-tick, DUM-DUM, DUM-DUM – I loved that. I loved too the sound of the monsoon rain on the corrugated roof of our verandah when I was tucked up in bed.

Spike Milligan

Forsan et haec olim meminisse iuvabit.

Perhaps, one day it will delight us
to remember these things.

Virgil

Nothing is ever lost or forgotten. Everything is stored within your soul in the temple of memory. Therefore, as an old person, you can happily go back and attend to your past time; you can return through the rooms of that temple, visit the days that you enjoyed and the times of difficulty where you grew and refined your self. In actual fact, old age as the harvest of life, is a time where your times and their fragments gather. Old age is a time of coming home to your deeper nature, of entering fully into the temple of your memory where all your vanished days are secretly gathered awaiting you.

John O'Donohue

Yet in this heart's most sacred place
Thou, thou alone, shalt dwell forever.
And still shall recollection trace
In fancy's mirror, ever near,
Each smile, each tear, upon that face –
Though lost to sight, to memory dear.

Thomas Moore

If time does anything, it deepens our grief. The longer we live, the more fully we become aware of who she was for us and the more intimately we experience what her love meant for us. Real deep love is, as you know, very unobtrusive, seemingly easy and obvious that we take it for granted. Therefore, it is often only in retrospect – or better, in memory – that we fully realise its power and depth.

Henri Nouwen

The top of the dresser – in the kitchen of the house where I lived for my first twelve years – was like a time machine. This was where the old nails and screwdrivers, putty, lamp-wicks and broken sharpening stones would end up. Its mystery had to do with its inaccessibility for me. When I managed to climb up there, the dusty newspaper on the putty, the worn-down grains on the sharpening stones, the bent nails, the singed ends of the wicks, the dust and stillness and rust – all suggested that these objects were living a kind of afterlife. They were not inert rubbish, but dormant energies. We read ourselves into our personal past by reading the significant images in our personal world.

Seamus Heaney

Being Thankful for ...

Health and Healing

O Lord, you have probed me and you know me;
you know when I sit and when I stand:
you understand my thoughts from afar.
My journeys and my rest you scrutinise;
with all my ways you are familiar.

If I take the wings of the dawn,
if I settle at the farthest limits of the sea,
Even there your hand shall guide me,
and your right hand hold me fast.

Truly you have formed my inmost being;
you knit me in my mother's womb.
I give you thanks that I am fearfully and
    wonderfully made;
wonderful are your works.

How weighty are your designs, O God;
how vast the sum of them.
Were I to recount them, they would outnumber
    the sands;
did I reach the end of them, I should still be with
    you.

Psalm 139

I have come to realise that every patient of mine, every newborn baby in every cell of its body, has a basic knowledge of how to survive and how to heal, that exceeds anything I shall ever know. That knowledge is the gift of God, who has made our bodies more perfectly than we could ever have devised.

Paul Brand

On the way to Jerusalem, Jesus travelled along the border between Samaria and Galilee. As he entered one of the villages, ten lepers came to meet him. They stood some way off and called to him, 'Jesus! Master! Take pity on us.' When he saw them he said, 'Go and show yourselves to the priests.' Now as they were going away they were cleansed. Finding himself cured, one of them turned back, praising God at the top of his voice and threw himself at the feet of Jesus and thanked him. The man was a Samaritan. This made Jesus say, 'Were not all ten made clean? The other nine, where are they? It seems that no one has come back to give praise to God, except this foreigner.' And he said to the man, 'Stand up and go on your way. Your faith has saved you.'

Luke 17:11–19

Look at our skin – something we might take for granted – and then stop and think of what it does; it encases the entire body; it stretches, breathes, blushes, pales, waterproofs, perspires, tingles, pains, itches, glows, glistens and acts as a frontline defence against the hordes of bacteria that relentlessly attack the human body. What a miracle!

Sean Boylan

———

Men go abroad to wonder at the height of mountains, at the huge waves of the sea, at the long courses of the rivers, at the vast compass of the ocean, at the circular motion of the stars – and they pass themselves by without wondering.

St Augustine

Listen to me, devout children, and blossom
like the rose that grows on the bank of a
    watercourse.
Give off a sweet smell like incense,
flower like the lily, spread your fragrance abroad,
sing a song of praise
blessing the Lord for all his works.

Ecclesiasticus 39:13–14

In my bay
Pre-meds done, chemo on the drip
I thank God for the wonder of it all
seed of the yew nourished by
soil inhabited by earthworms
sapling sprouting to
sun and rain
sheltering insects in
maturing tree
magnificent creation's indwelling powers
of healing, rebalancing, rebodying
I thank God for the one who drew out
these powers, was she – or he – someone
fired 'to make a difference'
to extract from the ancient tree
its secrets
stewarding God's manifold gifts
so that a woman such as I might be healed

Mary Redmond

Inside my human eye are 107,000,000 cells. Seven million are cones, each loaded to fire off a message to the brain when a few photons of light cross them. Cones give me the full band of colour awareness and because of them I can distinguish a thousand shades of colour. The other hundred million cells are rods, back-up cells for use in low light. When only rods are operating, I do not see colour, but I can distinguish a spectrum of light so broad that the brightest light I perceive is a billion times brighter than the dimmest.

Paul Brand

When one door of happiness closes, another one opens, but we look so long at the closed door that we do not see the one which has opened for us.

Helen Keller

I will extol you, O Lord, for you have drawn me
    up
and have not let my foes rejoice over me.
O Lord my God, I cried to you for help and you
    have healed me.

You have turned for me my mourning into
    dancing …
O Lord my God, I will give thanks to you for
    ever.

Psalm 30

Being Thankful for ...

Mentors

Gratitude is not only the greatest of virtues
but the parent of all others.

Cicero

————

A great mentor of mine was the parish priest of
Bansha when I was a child – Canon Hayes, who
founded Muintir na Tíre [a national voluntary
organisation dedicated to promoting the process
of community development]. I still remember his
sermons. The whole parish became involved in
what he believed in – a community as a social mix
of equals. This may seem normal now, but seventy
years ago it was revolutionary. All his philosophical
stuff about the danger of materialism, the need for
people to be in contact, to share their time and

gifts, to help the struggling, all of that left a mark on me and very much influenced me in my work.

Another great influence in my life is Jean Vanier, founder of the L'Arche organisation, which provides community living for the disabled and the broken in our society. Vanier gave up his comfortable life to seek out and befriend the marginalised and friendless. He is the true definition of a 'walking saint', simply because he practises what he preaches, recognising that 'man's most primal cry is to be loved'. I had the great honour of sharing a weekend with him in Derry some years ago. His words remain with me: 'To listen to another human being into a condition of disclosure is the greatest service you can bestow on a fellow human being.'

John Lonergan

I was twenty-one when I left the navy and went to a small community near Paris which was founded by a French Dominican called Thomas Philippe and that was a very deep experience. I came there both mature and immature. Mature, because I had assumed a lot of responsibility and done a lot of things in the navy – probably a lot more mature than many young people of the same age – but quite immature in my capacity to relate and from the point of view of my intellectual and cultural development. I was seeking to grow intellectually and spiritually.

I think Père Thomas brought together three elements – a mystical element, a real union with Jesus leading into silence; a whole vision of metaphysics and theology; and also a vision of the needs of young people, particularly in the period after World War II. He was a man who was very interested in people. Through these three elements, I was nourished and formed intellectually, metaphysically and theologically and I was led into a life of prayer. I finished my studies at the Catholic Institute in Paris and started teaching at St Michael's College in Toronto.

In 1963, I went to visit Père Thomas, who had become chaplain of a small institute for thirty men with mental disabilities. He had suggested that I come and meet his 'new friends'. I went to visit them with much fear and some misgivings, because I didn't know how to communicate with people who had a mental handicap. How do you speak with people who can't speak? And even if they did speak, what would we talk about? I was very touched by these men with all that was broken in them, their handicaps, their incapacities. Each one was thirsting for a relationship. Each was asking, 'Do you love me? Will you be my friend?' My students in philosophy wanted my head but not my heart. They were interested in the courses I could give them so that they could pass their exams and move on. They were not saying, 'Do you love me?'; they were saying, 'What can you give me to pass my exam?'

Père Thomas encouraged me to take two men from an asylum and live with them. Raphael had had meningitis when he was young and would fall over easily. Philippe had had encephalitis when he was young and had one paralysed leg and one paralysed arm; he also had a mental handicap, though he could speak well. We started living together – and so began the adventure of L'Arche.

Jean Vanier

I went initially to a Jesuit school in Paris and did very well academically. Our house in Paris was very much an open house. John O'Leary and Roger Casement came there, as did some Indian revolutionary leaders. My favourite visitor was the writer James Stephens. He was a great storyteller. He told me about his namesake, the Fenian leader: 'He wasn't small like me. He was a big, burly man. Once when police tried to arrest him, he lifted four of them in the air at once and escaped!' He would take me out to indulge in my passion for stamp collecting. He gave me a certain amount of money to spend and then sat in the corner of the shop reading while I made my choices. Then we went to Rumplemeyer's for ice cream and cake – and lots of stories from James Stephens. I idolised him. Yeats was a regular visitor too. We had a house by the sea in Normandy. Yeats bought me a kite and taught me to fly it. He was really good at it and probably enjoyed it more than me. I was too young at the time.

Sean McBride

I made no friends in boarding school, but there was one man in the school who became my mentor. He was my class master and also my house master and he taught me an enormous number of things, not just the subjects – Greek, Latin and ancient history – that he was teaching me. One morning after being in the school chapel, we returned to our class and were supposed to be translating Virgil or something terribly boring, when he said, 'Which of you can give me the name of the composer of the organ music that we heard this morning in chapel?' Dead silence. He said, 'This is disastrous. You are sixteen years of age. You have just listened to one of the most marvellous pieces of Bach that the world could ever hear and you don't even know it. We will not look at any Latin this morning. We will go back to my house and I will play you the kind of music that ought to be in your souls for ever more.'

This man opened my mind in a quite incredible way, and then he did something which had an amazing effect on my life. He made me sit the exam for Oxford, even though I was preparing to go to Trinity College, Dublin, where all my family had gone before me. In the end I went to Oxford and not to Trinity, thereby living in England and not Ireland. I don't know yet whether that was for good or for ill, but it certainly changed my life – and that man made it happen. In that desert, there was this wonderful prophet and I was very lucky that he latched on to me. He gave up his holidays, as so many dedicated teachers do, to take pupils on school trips, and in those days it was rare to go to the Continent, but he took us all off to the South of France, to look at Roman ruins and things like that. Not only did we see Roman ruins, but for the first time in my life I, a little Irish boy from the bogs of Kildare, began to understand the civilisation that exists in the Mediterranean – the smells, the scents, the wine and so on.

Charles Handy

———

Margaret or 'Peg' Kneeshaw was for many years Children's and Schools' Librarian for Dublin City Council and it was in that capacity that I got to know her in the mid-1960s. I was a young enthusiastic teacher in a huge school in the then sprawling new suburb of Finglas West. The school was bursting at the seams within a year or two of its opening. I taught in a room that had been purpose-built as a library but pressure for classroom space meant it was always used as a classroom during my seven years in that school. I fought a running but losing battle to have a properly established library for a school of one thousand pupils but the running joke was, 'The library has been shelved again'.

The positive side of the campaign was that I got to know Peg Kneeshaw. The Schools' Library

Department was on the corner of Wellington Quay – on the fourth floor – and from there Peg and her small dedicated staff serviced the library needs of Dublin city schools. It was an Aladdin's Cave to me – rows and stacks and shelves and jumbles and pyramids of wonderful books. When I failed to make a library out of the school library, Peg allowed me to take a classroom collection – eighty to one hundred books – which I could renew every so often.

I was in heaven – or at least its anteroom – every time I visited that top floor. Here I was introduced to a whole new burgeoning world of children's literature. Here I fumbled my way into the cinema with *Paddington Bear*, went tobogganing with Laura Ingalls Wilder of the *Little House on the Prairie*, wept with Granny Conroy as she visited Eilís Dillon's *Island of Horses*, trembled at the advance of Ted Hughes' *Iron Man*. And always the gentle proddings of Peg Kneeshaw guided me: 'Try this one! She's a wonderful writer! … That's a beautiful story for eight-year-olds.' In my attempts to open new worlds for the children of Finglas, a whole new world was being opened to me by this quiet, gentle and wise woman.

Ten years later, the library had at last become a library, but I had moved on. I was now in schools publishing, trying to compile English anthologies for senior primary standards. To whom did I turn? Peg Kneeshaw. Once again I was given the freedom of Wellington Quay to muse and choose, and always at my shoulder the gentle, guiding voice of Peg Kneeshaw – 'Seven to ten is the time when children are introduced to fantasy. There are some books which if children don't get them at this age they will never get them. I'm thinking of a classic like *Alice's Adventures in Wonderland*. If you don't read that at a certain age, you're always going to be too old or too young for it.'

Another decade later I had moved on once more – to broadcasting. In 1982 I produced a series called *Children Reading* – a guide for parents to the world of children's books. Once again, I drew on the wisdom and experience of Peg Kneeshaw. Peg introduced a whole generation of child readers to exciting new writers like Joan Lingard,

Philippa Pearce and Rosemary Sutcliff. Peg was a gentle and gracious lady who served her public in an unassuming but most dedicated way. To me she was a valued mentor through three different careers.

John Quinn

Paulo Freire has been a huge influence on my life. We became good friends and I translated his last, and in my opinion finest, book, *Pedagogy of Freedom*. Some phrases from the core of his thinking include: 'We have to talk about the obvious'; 'Don't go in with a ready-made project'; 'Be a fly on the wall – listen!'; 'Travel with people, not in front or behind'; 'Every teacher is also a learner'; 'Every learner is also a teacher'; 'Don't pretend that your story can imitate the story of someone else. Meet their story.'

Freire influenced, and was influenced by, Liberation Theology. You are not an indoctrinator, you are on a journey. That is the basic thing about the 'people of God' image. As a missionary, I see my role as trying to keep a community in a cohesive dynamic. There are many conflicts in a community and you become a reference point for dialogue, understanding, forgiveness. Basic communities have generated so much else, in terms of social awareness, in projects linked to the life of their faith. It really is a gospel of many dimensions.

Pat Clarke

Being Thankful for ...

Blessings

Let gratitude be the pillow upon which you kneel
to say your nightly prayer.

Maya Angelou

———

I felt it incumbent on myself to say a prayer. I
went on my knees, my hands clasped in prayer. My
expression is as if I've seen a vision.

Ronnie Delany, on winning the
Olympic 1,500 m title in Melbourne, 1956

Reflect upon your present blessings, of which every man has plenty, not on your past misfortunes, of which all men have some.

Charles Dickens

Whatever talent I have is God-given and I am thankful for that. It has given me a good life and enabled my wife, Barbara, and me to rear seven children. I never wanted to be a Hollywood star or a millionaire, just to do what I do well and to keep doing it for a living.

Frank Kelly

When I started counting my blessings my whole life turned around.

Willie Nelson

Now thank we all our God
With heart and hand and voices,
Who wondrous things has done,
In whom this world rejoices;
Who from our mother's arms
Has blessed us on our way
With countless gifts of love,
And still is ours today.

Martin Rinkart

———

It is only with gratitude that life becomes rich.

Dietrich Bonhoeffer

———

I never stop thanking God for all the graces you have received through Jesus Christ. I thank him that you have been enriched in so many ways, especially in your teachers and preachers.

1 Corinthians 1:4–6

I still go onto the stage up to the gills with nerves, but God pulls me through and for that I give thanks.

Maureen Potter

Acknowledging the good you already have in your life is the foundation for all abundance.

Eckhart Tolle

Let's rise and be thankful, for if we didn't learn a lot today, at least we may have learned a little. And if we didn't learn even a little, at least we didn't get sick. And if we did get sick, at least we didn't die. So let us all be thankful.

Buddhist Teaching

When upon life's billows you are tempest-toss'd
When you are discouraged, thinking all is lost,
Count your many blessings, name them one by
   one
And it will surprise you what the Lord had done.

So, amid the conflict, whether great or small
Do not be discouraged, God is over all;
Count your many blessings, angels will attend,
Help and comfort give you to your journey's end.

Johnson Oatman, Jr

Envoi

It is entirely fitting that I conclude this book with a poem by the woman to whose memory it is dedicated. On her diagnosis with breast cancer, Mary Redmond discovered a wonderful force within her – we can be ill, yet whole. Under her married name, Mary Ussher, she compiled *The Pink Ribbon Path*, an anthology of prayers, reflections and meditations for women with breast cancer. It is 'a path for healing, for living, for hope, a journey which once embarked upon becomes a daily joy'.

What can I render to the Lord
For all that he has
Rendered unto me.

For the continuing gift of life
For sparing and transforming it
I thank you.

For each new sunrise
And birdsong, your liturgy,
I thank you.

For sleeping to the gift of rest
And rising to the gift of life
I thank you.

For winter-flowering cherry blossom,
My father's rose, and lavender
I thank you.

For every cell and particle
Restored to your healing
I thank you.

For hair and nails re-grown
And new peace in my deepest core
I thank you.

For love of husband, child, mother
Siblings, spouses
I thank you.

For support of pink sisters
And tireless friends along the way
I thank you.

For nurses, doctors, their infusions
Cheery women who brought the tea
I thank you.

For every tear in near despair
The love in your Cross
I thank you.

For help in the battle
Between faith and fear
I thank you.

Envoi / 183

For having heard and answered me
Especially when I could not pray
I thank you.

For passage to a new life
Beyond all imagining
I thank you.

For new lens to discern
'success' and 'worry'
I thank you.

For Your Spirit's awesome presence
O uncreated One
I thank you.

For the music of your silence
Sweetest surrender
I thank you.

And I pray that all women
on the Pink Ribbon Path
may find and love you, Lord.
That, by your grace,

if I am again afflicted
with this disease
I may remain on the Path.
That through Mary my prayers may be
an instrument of hope;
and that one day, O God of life,
breast cancer will be overcome.

Mary Redmond

———

The depths of the theory of thanks are bottomless,
are spirit, are love.

Mary Redmond

———

Mary Redmond died on Easter Monday,
6 April 2015.

Contributors

ANGELOU, MAYA (1928–2014): American writer
and civil rights activist.

ANGELUS SILESIUS, JOHANN (1624–77): German
priest, poet and mystic.

AUGUSTINE, ST (AD 354–430): Bishop, theologian
and philosopher from North Africa.

AUSTEN, JANE (1775–1817): English novelist.

BARTH, KARL (1886–1968): Swiss Protestant
theologian.

BERRY, WENDELL (b. 1934): American novelist,
poet and environmental activist.

BONHOEFFER, DIETRICH (1906–45): German
writer and theologian.

Boylan, Clare (1948–2006): Irish writer and journalist.

Boylan, Sean (b. 1949): Herbalist and former Gaelic football manager.

Brady, Eilís (1927–2007): Author of *All in! All in!: a selection of Dublin children's traditional street-games with rhymes and music* (Dublin: Four Courts Press, 1975).

Brand, Paul (1914–2003): American surgeon. Pioneer in treatment of leprosy.

Browning, Elizabeth Barrett (1806–61): English poet. Wife of Robert Browning.

Burton, Richard (1925–84): Welsh stage and screen actor.

Carver, Raymond (1938–88): American short-story writer and poet.

CAVAFY, CONSTANTINE (1863–1933): Greek poet and journalist.

CHESTERTON, GILBERT KEITH (1874–1936): English writer, dramatist and philosopher.

CICERO, MARCUS TULLIUS (106–43 BC): Roman politician, writer and orator.

CLARKE, PAT: Spiritan priest who has worked among the poor in Brazil for over forty years.

COADY, MICHAEL (b. 1939): Irish poet, writer and local historian.

COOLEY, MIKE (b. 1934): Irish engineer, trade union activist and writer.

COON COME, MATTHEW (b. 1956): Canadian politician and activist on behalf of indigenous people.

CROZIER, WILLIAM (1930–2011): Irish-Scots artist.

DALY, CAHAL (1917–2009): Irish cardinal, theologian and writer.

DE BARRA, EIBHLÍS (d. 2006): Cork-born storyteller and writer.

DELANY, RONNIE (b. 1935): Irish athlete, winner of gold medal, 1500 m, at Melbourne Olympics 1956.

DEVLIN, POLLY (b. 1941): Tyrone-born writer and broadcaster.

DICKENS, CHARLES (1812–70): English novelist and social critic.

DONLON, PATRICIA (b. 1943): Former Director of the National Library of Ireland and specialist in children's books.

ECKHART, MEISTER (c. 1260–1328): German theologian and philosopher.

EINSTEIN, ALBERT (1879–1955): German
physicist.

EMERSON, RALPH WALDO (1803–82): American
philosopher, poet and essayist.

FITZGERALD, GARRET (1926–2011): Irish
politician. Former taoiseach of Ireland.

GRAHAM, PADDY (b. 1943): Westmeath-born
artist. Member of Aosdána.

GREGORY, ANNE (1911–2008) & CATHERINE
(1913–2006): Granddaughters of Lady Gregory of
Coole Park, where they grew up.

GURNEY, DOROTHY FRANCES (1858–1932):
English poet and hymn-writer.

HANDY, CHARLES (b. 1932): Kildare-born writer,
broadcaster and social philosopher.

HEANEY, SEAMUS (1939–2013): Derry-born poet, translator, playwright. Winner of the Nobel Prize 1995.

HEDERMAN, MARK PATRICK (b. 1944): Benedictine monk. Former Abbot of Glenstal Abbey, Co. Limerick. Writer and lecturer.

HOPKINS, GERARD MANLEY (1844–89): English poet and Jesuit priest. Buried in Glasnevin Cemetery.

HUME, JOHN (b. 1937): Derry-born politician. Founder of the Social Democratic and Labour Party. Co-winner of Nobel Prize 1998.

KAGGE, ERLING (b. 1963): Norwegian explorer and writer.

KAVANAGH, PATRICK (1904–67): Monaghan-born poet and novelist.

KELLER, HELEN (1880–1968): American deaf-blind author and political activist.

KELLY, FRANK (1938–2016): Irish actor on radio, television, stage and screen.

KENNELLY, BRENDAN (b. 1936): Kerry-born poet and novelist. Professor Emeritus of Trinity College, Dublin.

KILCOYNE, PHYLLIS: Sligo-born nun, member of the Mercy Order. Former teacher and school principal.

KILMER, JOYCE (1886–1918): American poet and critic. Killed in action in France during World War I.

LEAHY, ALICE (b. 1941): Former nurse who founded TRUST, a befriending social and health service for homeless people.

LEDWIDGE, FRANCIS (1887–1917): Meath-born 'poet of the blackbird'. Killed in action in Ypres during World War I.

LEONARD, HUGH (1926–2009): Dublin-born playwright and television writer.

LETTS, WINIFRED MARY (1882–1972): Poet, novelist and playwright who, though born in England, spent most of her life in Ireland.

LEWIS, NAOMI (1911–2009): English poet, critic and writer for children.

LINNEY, GORDON (b. 1939): Anglican priest and writer. Former archdeacon of Dublin.

LONERGAN, JOHN (b. 1948): Tipperary-born former governor of Mountjoy Prison, Dublin. Writer and leadership speaker.

McBRIDE, SEAN (1904–88): Irish politician. Founder of Clann na Poblachta party. Winner of Nobel Peace Prize in 1974.

McCABE, EUGENE (b. 1930): Irish novelist, playwright, television screenwriter, farmer.

McGAHERN, JOHN (1934–2006): Leitrim-born novelist and short-story writer.

McGOUGH, ROGER (b. 1937): Liverpool-born poet, broadcaster, children's author.

McKENNA, TP (1929–2011): Cavan-born actor on stage, screen and television.

MILLIGAN, SPIKE (1918–2002): Comedian, writer, poet, actor.

MONAHAN, PEGG: Stage and radio actress. Former member of RTÉ Repertory Company.

MOORE, THOMAS (1779–1852): Dublin-born poet, singer, songwriter.

MORIARTY, JOHN (1938–2007): Kerry-born writer and philosopher.

MOTHER TERESA (1910–97): Albanian-born nun who devoted her life to the poor of Calcutta. Canonised in 2016.

MURRAY, MARIE: Clinical psychologist, journalist, author and broadcaster.

NELSON, WILLIE (b. 1933): American musician, singer, songwriter, poet.

NIETZSCHE, FRIEDRICH (1844–1900): German philosopher, scholar, poet.

NOUWEN, HENRI (1932–96): Dutch Catholic priest, writer, theologian.

OATMAN, JOHNSON, JR (1856–1922): American Methodist minister and hymn-writer.

O'CALLAGHAN, MIRIAM (b. 1960): Dublin-born television and radio presenter.

O'DONNELL, MARIE-LOUISE (b. 1952): Member of the Irish Senate. Broadcaster and lecturer.

O'DONOHUE, JOHN (1956–2008): Clare-born philosopher, poet, priest and writer on Celtic spirituality.

O'FAOLÁIN, SEÁN (1900–91): Cork-born short-story writer and biographer.

O'HARA, MARY (b. 1935): Sligo-born singer and harpist.

PLUNKETT, JAMES (1920–2003): Dublin-born short-story writer and novelist.

PLUNKETT, JOSEPH MARY (1887–1916): Poet, one of the leaders of the 1916 Rising. Executed in Kilmainham Gaol.

POPE, ALEXANDER (1688–1744): English poet and satirist.

POPE FRANCIS (b. 1936): Argentina-born pope, head of the Catholic Church. Jesuit priest and former archbishop of Buenos Aires.

POTTER, MAUREEN (1925–2004): Dublin-born comedian, actor and singer.

QUINN, JOHN (b. 1941): Meath-born writer and former radio broadcaster.

REDMOND, MARY (1951–2015): Lawyer, academic, writer and founder of the Irish Hospice Foundation.

REYNOLDS, MARY (b. 1974): Wexford-born gardener, landscape-designer and writer.

RINKART, MARTIN (1586–1649): German
Lutheran clergyman and hymn-writer.

SCHWEITZER, ALBERT (1875–1965): French-born
theologian, writer, humanitarian and physician.

SHAKESPEARE, WILLIAM (1564–1616): English
playwright, poet and actor.

SIGERSON SHORTER, DORA (1866–1918): Dublin-
born poet and sculptor.

SUTCLIFF, ROSEMARY (1920–92): English writer
of historical fiction and retellings of myths and
legends.

TAYLOR, ALICE (b. 1938): Cork-born writer and
novelist.

TOLLE, ECKHART (b. 1948): German-born
spiritual writer.

VANIER, JEAN (b. 1928): Canadian-born Catholic philosopher and humanitarian. Founder of L'Arche Organisation.

VIRGIL [PUBLIUS VERGILIUS MARO] (70–19 BC): Roman poet, best known for the epic poem the *Aeneid*.

WATERS, JOHN (b. 1955): Roscommon-born journalist and writer.

WHITMAN, WALT (1819–92): American poet, essayist and journalist.

WILDER, THORNTON (1897–1975): American playwright and novelist.

WILSON, GORDON (1927–95): Leitrim-born peace campaigner following the death of his daughter Marie in the 1987 Enniskillen bombing.

WILSON, JOAN: Wife of Gordon Wilson. Musician and writer.

Sources

INTRODUCTION: Patrick Kavanagh, 'Question to Life', *Collected Poems*, edited by Antoinette Quinn (Allen Lane, 2004), by kind permission of the Trustees of the Estate of the late Katherine B. Kavanagh, through the Jonathan Williams Literary Agency. THE WORLD ABOUT US: Erling Kagge, *Silence: In the Age of Noise*, London: Penguin, 2017. Wendell Berry, 'The Peace of Wild Things', *The Selected Poems of Wendell Berry*, Berkeley, CA: Counterpoint Press, 1999. St Augustine, *The Book of Nature*, De Civit. Dei, Book XVI. Gerard Manley Hopkins, 'God's Grandeur', *Gerard Manley Hopkins: Poems and Prose*, Penguin Classics, 1985. Joyce Kilmer, 'Trees', *Trees and Other Poems*, New York: Doubleday Doran and Co., 1914, p. 18. Matthew Coon Come, 'Listening to the People', in *The Curious Mind: Twenty-Five Years of John Quinn Radio Programmes*, Dublin: Veritas, 2009, pp. 213–15. Dorothy Frances Gurney, 'God's Garden', *Poems by Dorothy Frances Gurney*, London: Country Life, 1913. Gerard Manley Hopkins, 'Pied Beauty', *Poems and Prose*, 1985. Winifred M. Letts, 'A Soft Day', *Songs from Leinster*, London: Smith, Elder and Co., 1913. Gerard Manley Hopkins, 'Inversnaid', *Poems and Prose*. A LOVING GOD: Pope Francis, *Homily of His Holiness Pope Francis*, Apostolic Journey to Sri Lanka and the Philippines, Tacloban International Airport, 17 January 2015. Gordon Wilson, 'Finding Forgiveness', in *The Curious Mind*, pp. 69–71. Quoting John G. Whittier, 'O Brother Man', 1848. Joan Wilson, in John Quinn (ed.), *CREDO: Personal Testimonies of Faith*, Dublin: Veritas, 2014, pp. 161–8. Joseph Mary Plunkett, 'I See His Blood upon the Rose', *The Poems of Joseph Mary Plunkett*, Dublin:

Talbot Press, 1919. **BOOKS:** Jane Austen, *Northanger Abbey*, 1816. Hugh Leonard, 'In Praise of Reading', in *The Curious Mind*, pp. 24–7. Patricia Donlon, 'Cornelius Rabbit and Other Friends', in *The Curious Mind*, pp. 192–6. Naomi Lewis quoted by Anne Fine, 'And So Do Big Babies …', in *The Curious Mind*, pp. 83–5. Cardinal Cahal Daly, 'A Classical Education', in *The Curious Mind*, pp. 243–5. John McGahern, 'The Odd Couple', in *The Curious Mind*, pp. 325–6. Elizabeth Barrett Browning, 'The Library in the Garret', *Aurora Leigh*, 1957. **THE GIFT OF LOVE:** William Shakespeare, 'Sonnet 29'. John Quinn, *Letters to Olive: Sea of Love, Sea of Loss: Seed of Love, Seed of Life*, Dublin: Veritas, 2011. Mary Redmond, in *CREDO*, pp. 137–43. Charles Handy, 'Seven Handy Propositions', in *The Curious Mind*, pp. 326–7. Rosemary Sutcliff, 'Blue Remembered Hills', in *The Curious Mind*, pp. 98–101. Marie Murray, 'The Pain of Cupid's Bow', *The Irish Times*, 14 February 2006. Seamus Heaney, 'Album', *Human Chain*, London: Faber and Faber, 2010. Garret FitzGerald, 'College Life and Love', in *The Curious Mind*, pp. 298–9. Thomas Moore, ''Tis All for Thee', *The Poetical Works of Thomas Moore*, New York: D. Appleton & Company, 1846. Henri Nouwen, *A Letter of Consolation*, San Francisco: HarperCollins, 2009, p. 32. Mary O'Hara, in *CREDO*, pp. 121–8. Eugene McCabe, 'For Margot for a Lifetime', epigraph of *Heaven Lies about Us*, London: Bloomsbury, 2004. Raymond Carver, 'Letter to Leonard Russell', in Shaun Usher (ed.), *More Letters of Note: Correspondence Deserving of a Wider Audience*, Edinburgh: Canongate Books Ltd, 2015. John O'Donohue, *Anam Cara: Spiritual Wisdom from the Celtic World*, London:

Bantam Books, 2011. A GIFTED TEACHER: TP McKenna, 'Vincent', in *The Curious Mind*, pp. 317–18. Michael D. Higgins, 'To School Through Poetry', in *The Curious Mind*, pp. 302–3. Mike Cooley, in John Quinn, *My Education*, Dublin: Town House, 1997. Brendan Kennelly, in *My Education*. SILENCE, SOLITUDE – AND DOING NOTHING: Mary O'Hara, in *CREDO*, pp. 121–8. Garret FitzGerald, 'College Life and Love', in *The Curious Mind*, pp. 298–9. Brendan Kennelly, in *My Education*. Alice Leahy, in *CREDO*, pp. 81–7. Seán O'Faoláin, *Vive-Moi! An Autobiography*, Little Brown, 1964. John O'Donohue, *Walking on the Pastures of Wonder: In Conversation with John Quinn*, Dublin: Veritas, 2015. Paddy Graham, 'On County Westmeath', in John Quinn (ed.), *This Place Speaks to Me: An Anthology of People and Places*, Dublin: Veritas, 2016, pp. 85–90. Alice Taylor, in *CREDO*, pp. 145–51. PARENTS: John Hume, in *My Education*. Francis Ledwidge, 'My Mother', *The Complete Poems of Francis Ledwidge*, London: Herbert Jenkins, 1919. Clare Boylan, in John Quinn (ed.), *A Portrait of the Artist as a Young Girl*, Methuen, 1987. Seamus Heaney, in *My Education*. Seamus Heaney, 'When all the others were away at Mass', 'Clearances III', *Opened Ground: Poems 1966–1996*, London: Faber and Faber, 1998. Anne & Catherine Gregory, 'Grandma, Mr Yeats and GBS', in *The Curious Mind*, pp. 45–7. EVERYDAY THINGS: Dora Sigerson Shorter, 'I Want to Talk to Thee of Little Things'. Miriam O'Callaghan, quoted in 'Stressbusters – Well-Known Irish Personalities on How to Manage Stress', *Sunday Independent Life Magazine*, 8 January 2018. Angelus Silesius, 'Without Why'. Patrick Kavanagh, 'The Long

Garden', *Collected Poems*. Mary Redmond, 'This, My Everyday', *The Pink Ribbon Path*, Dublin: The Columba Press, 2013, p. 44. **THE GIFT OF FAITH**: Mark Patrick Hederman, in *CREDO*, pp. 59–65. Michael Coady, in *CREDO*, pp. 43–50. John Waters, in *CREDO*, pp. 153–9. Gordon Linney, in *CREDO*, pp. 89–95. Sean Boylan, in *CREDO*, pp. 19–26. Mary O'Hara, in *CREDO*, pp. 121–8. Mary Redmond, in *CREDO*, pp. 137–43. **OUR OWN PLACE**: Polly Devlin, 'On Ardboe', in *This Place Speaks to Me*, pp. 91–7. James Plunkett, 'A Child of Strumpet City', in *The Curious Mind*, pp. 54–6. Paddy Graham, 'On County Westmeath', in *This Place Speaks to Me*, pp. 85–90. Eilís Brady, 'Paradise Lost', in *The Curious Mind*, pp. 284–6. Michael Coady, 'On Carrick-on-Suir', in *This Place Speaks to Me*, pp. 131–41. Eibhlís de Barra, 'On the Coal Quay, Cork', in *This Place Speaks to Me*, pp. 25–30. **CONTENTMENT**: John Moriarty, *Nostos: An Autobiography*, Dublin: Lilliput Press, 2011, p. 491. Patrick Kavanagh, 'Ploughman', *Collected Poems*. John McGahern, *Memoir*, London: Faber and Faber, 2005, p. 809. Gilbert Keith Chesterton, *A Short History of England*, 1917. Phyllis Kilcoyne, in *CREDO*, pp. 73–9. Alexander Pope, 'Ode on Solitude', 1700. Mary Reynolds, *The Garden Awakening: Designs to Nurture Our Land and Ourselves*, Cambridge: Green Books, 2016. **THE GIFT OF MEMORY**: Walt Whitman, 'Continuities', *Leaves of Grass*, Philadelphia: David McKay, 1891–2. St Augustine, *Confessions*, Book X. Marie-Louise O'Donnell, 'Foreword', in *This Place Speaks to Me*, pp. 9–13. Spike Milligan, 'An Indian Boyhood', in *The Curious Mind*, pp. 19–22. Virgil, *Aeneid*. John O'Donohue,

Anam Cara. Thomas Moore, 'Though Lost To Sight, To Memory Dear'. Henri Nouwen, *A Sorrow Shared: A Combined Edition of the Nouwen Classics In Memoriam and A Letter of Consolation*, Indiana: Ava Maria Press, 2010, p. 57. Seamus Heaney, 'A Sense of the Past', in *The Curious Mind*, pp. 138–41. HEALTH AND HEALING: Paul Brand, Philip Yancey and Dr Paul Brand, *Fearfully and Wonderfully Made*, Michigan: Zondervan Publishing House, 1980. Sean Boylan, in *CREDO*, pp. 19–26. St Augustine, *Confessions*. Mary Redmond, 'Thoughts', *The Pink Ribbon Path*, p. 62. Paul Brand, *Fearfully and Wonderfully Made*, p. 22. MENTORS: John Lonergan, in *CREDO*, pp. 97–103. Jean Vanier, in *My Education*. Sean McBride, 'Flying Kites with Mr Yeats', in *The Curious Mind*, pp. 69–71. Charles Handy, in *My Education*. John Quinn, 'Remembering Peg', in *The Curious Mind*, pp. 311–12. Pat Clarke, in *CREDO*, 2014, pp. 35–41. BLESSINGS: Ronnie Delany, quoted in Larry Ryan, 'Remembering Ronnie Delany's "great day"', *Irish Examiner*, 30 November 2016. Frank Kelly, in *CREDO*, pp. 67–72. Maureen Potter, in *My Education*. Buddhist Teaching, quoted in Leo Buscaglia, *Born for Love: Reflections on Loving*, New York: Fawcett Books, 1992, p. 102. ENVOI: Mary Redmond, 'Thanksgiving', *The Pink Ribbon Path*, p. 104.